BACKYARD WILDLIFE
Salamanders

By Megan Borgert-Spaniol

BLASTOFF! READERS

BELLWETHER MEDIA • MINNEAPOLIS, MN

Note to Librarians, Teachers, and Parents:

Blastoff! Readers are carefully developed by literacy experts and combine standards-based content with developmentally appropriate text.

Level 1 provides the most support through repetition of high-frequency words, light text, predictable sentence patterns, and strong visual support.

Level 2 offers early readers a bit more challenge through varied simple sentences, increased text load, and less repetition of high-frequency words.

Level 3 advances early-fluent readers toward fluency through increased text and concept load, less reliance on visuals, longer sentences, and more literary language.

Level 4 builds reading stamina by providing more text per page, increased use of punctuation, greater variation in sentence patterns, and increasingly challenging vocabulary.

Level 5 encourages children to move from "learning to read" to "reading to learn" by providing even more text, varied writing styles, and less familiar topics.

Whichever book is right for your reader, Blastoff! Readers are the perfect books to build confidence and encourage a love of reading that will last a lifetime!

This edition first published in 2012 by Bellwether Media, Inc.

No part of this publication may be reproduced in whole or in part without written permission of the publisher. For information regarding permission, write to Bellwether Media, Inc., Attention: Permissions Department, 5357 Penn Avenue South, Minneapolis, MN 55419.

Library of Congress Cataloging-in-Publication Data
Borgert-Spaniol, Megan, 1989-
  Salamanders / by Megan Borgert-Spaniol.
    p. cm. – (Blastoff! Readers. backyard wildlife)
  Includes bibliographical references and index.
  Summary: "Developed by literacy experts for students in kindergarten through grade three, this book introduces salamanders to young readers through leveled text and related photos"–Provided by publisher.
  ISBN 978-1-60014-723-4 (hardcover : alk. paper)
  1. Salamanders–Juvenile literature. I. Title.
  QL668.C2B66 2012
  597.8'5–dc23   2011028871

Printed in the United States of America, North Mankato, MN.

010112   1207

Contents

Salamanders are **amphibians** with tails. They have long bodies and short legs.

Most salamanders
breathe through
their skin.

They must keep their skin wet and cool. They can die if they get too dry or hot.

9

Salamanders **shed** their skin as they grow. They often eat the old skin.

Most salamanders
live in forests
near water.
They find shade
under rocks
and logs.

Salamanders do not move very fast. They eat slow animals like worms, slugs, and snails.

Salamanders grab **prey** with their sharp teeth. Some catch quick prey with their tongues.

Salamanders have **poison** on their skin. It protects them from **predators**.

Some salamanders shed their tails to escape an attack. The tail stays and the salamander runs away. Bye tail!

Glossary

amphibians—animals that live both on land and in water

poison—something that can harm or kill

predators—animals that hunt other animals for food

prey—animals that are hunted by other animals for food

shed—to drop or let fall off; salamanders shed their skin as they grow; they shed their tails to escape predators.

To Learn More

AT THE LIBRARY

Himmelman, John. *A Salamander's Life*. New York, N.Y.: Children's Press, 1998.

Lamstein, Sarah. *Big Night for Salamanders*. Honesdale, Pa.: Boyds Mills Press, 2010.

Mazer, Anne. *The Salamander Room*. New York, N.Y.: Knopf, 1991.

ON THE WEB

Learning more about salamanders is as easy as 1, 2, 3.

1. Go to www.factsurfer.com.

2. Enter "salamanders" into the search box.

3. Click the "Surf" button and you will see a list of related Web sites.

With factsurfer.com, finding more information is just a click away.

Index

The images in this book are reproduced through the courtesy of: Jack Goldfarb / Photolibrary, front cover; S & D & K Maslowski / Minden Pictures, p. 5; Maximilian Weinzierl / Alamy, p. 7; blickwinkel/Linke / Alamy, p. 9; Anton Luhr / Photolibrary, p. 11; Henry Wilson, pp. 13, 15 (left & right), 19; Susan Yates, p. 15; Rauschenbach Rauschenbach / Photolibrary, p. 17; Michel Rauch / Photolibrary, p. 21.
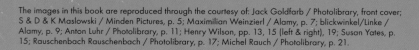